THE MILLION DOLLAR HOLE

ALSO BY MICHAEL CASEY

Obscenities

Millrat

THE
MILLION DOLLAR HOLE

MICHAEL CASEY

ORCHISES
Washington
2001

Library of Congress Cataloging in Publication Data

Casey, Michael (1947-   ).
The million dollar hole / Michael Casey.
p. cm.
ISBN 0-914061-86-0 (alk.) $12.95
1. Soldiers—Poetry I. Title.

PS3553.A7934 M54 2001
811'.54—dc21   00-039155

•

This is a work of fiction: the characters in it are not real people, and any similarity
or resemblance to a real person is wholly unintended and coincidental.

•

ACKNOWLEDGEMENTS
Thanks to these publications that initially printed the following poems:

Ararat	two blond honeys
	outpatient clinic
The Boston Phoenix	Manwarring's defenestration
Buffalo Vortex	south gate
The Chattahoochee Review	demonstrator post
The Ohio Review	black red purple dead
	Croft uncentered
Pomegranate Press Broadside Series	my brother-in-law and me
Prairie Schooner	AG Levy
	bus stop
	main gate
	Sp/4 West
Thorny Locust	463 Military Police Company

Manufactured in the United States of America

Orchises Press
P. O. Box 20602
Alexandria, Virginia
22320-1602

G6E4C2A

for

Stanley Kunitz

TABLE OF CONTENTS

main gate

the bus driver is furious
but I am bored
I stop the bus
and avoid the rolling Pepsi can
I speak with a command voice
ID cards and passes please
one troop shows me an ID but does not have a pass
my sergeant gave me a two ten verbal pass
and I got to give you this speech I says
you are under apprehension for attempted AWOL
I must advise you of your rights
under Article Thirty-one
of the Uniform Code of Military Justice
you have the right to remain silent
and anything you say may be used
against you at trial by courts martial
you have a right to an attorney
either civilian or military
however a civilian attorney
would be at your own expense
you have to come with me now
the girl with him begins to cry
what am I going to do
and I say
I have no jurisdiction over you miss
about a week later I figure out
she's talking to the troop and not to me
the willy had slash scars on his wrists
oh I catch on so quick

permanent party

the off base movie house was the Kozee Arts
and it had films there
like the hula dancer and the beach ball
and the legend of the master beater
there were always fights there
the woman at the ticket booth
would usually wear low cut outfits
and often some troop
would say something not nice
the owner of the theater biffs him
over the head with a metal pipe
not only willies but the sergeants
and clerks who made the fort run
trainees would get fractures
but also the permanent party
running the fort you know
the Swiss fort we run like clockwork
so the Provost Marshal
has a little talk with the owner
the MP school stick time lecture
don't hit nobody on the haid
hit the clavicle the collarbone
the guy'll be helpless and hurting
and back at work quicker without brain damage
the idea of having the woman
wear a bulky sweatshirt
never appears to nobody

no Grant

no Grant
now that hurt Grant
quit it will ya
aahh I promise Grant
I won't do it again
ouch promise on a Bible
I'll never call ya that honest
ya hurting me Grant
I'll never call ya that again
won't never gainsay you
hind your back or nothin
never even think it
won't never call ya moose again

MOOSE

brothers

the CI guy slithers out of his hole
walks quick without moving arms
likes to talk to the desk sergeant
about girls
some of us left jobs or schools
to get into this man's army
but Gregarian left a monastery
it's great you like doing laundry he said
the CI guy enjoys
grossing Greg out
talking how well he is doing
he complains but once
he had the sun burn lotion
in his hand and her bra strap undone
and that was as far as he could get
he goes back to his office
and Gregarian goes
ah shut up

company has two clerks now

got a new one
so what they do?
there's not enough work for one clerk
let lone two
they put one to work
making the outside company billboard
clerk two knows shit about building billboards
knows shit about building anything
brick layer Canney from Hartford
sees the shitty job
clerk two is doing
so Canney works making the bulletin board
on his own time
like there's nothing else to do
in the middle of Missouri
there isn't
he pays his own money
for a deelivery of fine sand
look at this old sand Case
too coarse too coarse
oh the Irish work ethic
oh the dumb shit

OFF-LIMITS & OUT-OF-BOUNDS

GREEN HILL SOCIAL CLUB, ALIAS GREEN
HILL NITE CLUB, HILLTOP COUNTRY CLUB,
HILLTOP CAFE, HILLTOP RESTAURANT,
ELLAR'S CAFE, SCOBY'S CAFE, SCOBY'S
BAR, SCOBY'S TAVERN, GOLD NUGGET
SOCIAL CLUB, BLACK AND WHITE CAFE
and all buildings and trailers adjacent thereto
at juncture of Route Two, Highway 28, Dixon, Missouri

Charlie Green from Lowell Tech and I parked near here
to drink beer and some guys in a white Cadillac stopped by
to invite us to a barbecue at the Black and White Social Club
to which the girls from the Big Daddy-B Cafe had moved.
Outside that building Town Patrol nabbed one guy and
his friend ran out half dressed and they nabbed him too.
A guy from FLW is in a coma at the hospital from a knife fight
there, slashed on forehead down between the eyes
to the diagonal cheek; they think he will be blind if he lives.

one lifeguard, rescued

Hernandez lucked out
and along with Reyes
had to check out the incident
at the WAC shack
the middle of the night
the middle of the summer
girls in skimpy PJ's
with shovels and rakes
and even a grass scythe
a willie got caught
climbing up the fire escape
and the Spanish Soul patrol
had to rescue his ass from all the girls
dude claimed he was the lifeguard

back up

You heard rumors that she went with officers, quietly, secretly so that no one would notice. But still Carl Hernandez gathers up his guts, asks her out, and she says OK. Carl's scared though. The WAC shack. It is like a sorority there and the first sergeant the mother superior. Carl has to get by her and she is really scary. So no, I did not go out on a date with them but I did go to the WAC shack. I was back up, the pretense being that he was driving and giving me a ride back to the pee barracks on the stockade hill. The WAC first sergeant accuses; she yells, who do you want to see? You are calling for who? Who is it you're here for? No answer from Carl, too busy shifting weight, one foot to the other. He finally mutters something, but she is yelling too loud. What is her name? And Carl gives his name. It was really funny but I was so embarrassed for him, I walked out. I walked back to the pee barracks. It was only two miles away.

report of pandering

the desk clerk Tooty
has to type it up on the blotter
report of pandering
what kind of fucking word is that?
and Gregarian goes   exactly

Gregarian the desk sergeant
was in a monastery
got out and was drafted
so how the fuck does he know
what that word means
I'll get him later about that

Outpatient Clinic, General Wood Hospital

the provost marshal
would send a patrol car to OPC
for lots of things animal bites
traffic accidents
wife beatings
the most common
but there were suicides too
and attempts at it poisonings say
and with a force for a giraffe's throat
Nurse Jones would push a tube
down a willie's throat
she was the nicest lieutenant nurse
at the General Leonard Wood Army Hospital
but she said she spends too much time and effort
trying to make people live
to have any sympathy for a dink
attempting the opposite
the real ones never made it
deep razor cuts
gunshot or hanging
but there were always
some overdoses of aspirins
one willie poisoned himself drinking Brasso
and at the company orderly room
where we picked him up he's in agony
blaming the sergeants
for not calling the police sooner
but at the OPC
as they're ready to pump out his stomach
he is asking Nurse Jones
if officers can date enlisteds

Nurse Jones did not answer
but with an ill humor
she pumped out his guts
she had fun with that one

demonstrator post

judo instructor at MP school say
near the end of the class
OK this is the last move
of the block hour instruction
slam your partner into that dust
centrifugate his ass
his stomach to the top of his brains
lying sonbitch
say in country is nothing
you walk on tippytoe
just one year and you come back
say wis nothing me rough me tough
lying sonbitch
then he say
no no that not the last move
it now your partner turn
slam your gut into the mud
remember the fifth step
my personal invention
when the opponent on the ground
you pull the hair out of his armpit

black red purple dead

insulted the next to last time by the cook
the troop runs back to the barracks
and tears apart his bunk
not just the mattress and blankets
but the actual frame
grabs the connecting pipe
the bunk adapter
and runs to the mess hall
he clubs the cook fierce
he really gets even
until the cookie
butcher knifes his heart
the troop falls
against and bites the cook's shoulder
I saw the scar
it looked sort of nice
the colors you know
like a kind of flower

bringing the witness

from the back of the cruiser
he asks me what happened
  at a time like that
I am supposed to keep quiet
I should say I don't know
I should say nothing
what I do? I tell him
  he's dead
and the cruiser gets real quiet
Wesley driving taps the dash three times
I add
  he was dead before he got to the hospital
Brother Wesley taps the dash board again
he asks me later
  didn't you hear me tap the first time?

Wesley

Wesley hits his head
against the steering wheel
hard but just once
and then hauls for an address
enlisted married quarters
outside they call these places hovels
says Wesley
  I know this address
  this the biggest man I ever saw
  always beatin hard on his wife
  we gonna walk in carrying
and Wesley steels up
not exactly talking to hisself
or to me but rather
to the addressee in advance
  I'll pop ya man I'll pop ya
the rehearsal? not needed
the man's huge
but he on the floor
out like flint
and his lady
albeit teensy tinesy's
holding a heavy and metal
most huge smoothing iron

town patrol

day times we had nothing better to do
than to catch lifers trying
to go into the grocery store
while wearing fatigues
a uniform violation off base at Wood
a Ford station wagon
stops in front of the grocery
red sticker NCO on the bumper
got one says my partner
but the driver of the wagon
before he gets out of the wagon
looks around him
and sees the MP car
starts up his wagon again and drives alongside
our Chevy Two cruiser
lowering the window he asks us
　you were gonna give me a DR
　because a wearin fattigoos?
　this is correct says my partner
and the sergeant drives off
partner explains it all to me
　old army called fatigues fattygoos
　and they were so ignorant
　they used to wear brown shoes

two blond honeys

there was a carnival on base
coincidentally just after the monthly pay day
and all kinds of cars were incoming even
after 5 PM and then outgoing after 11 PM
around midnight a blue gray Shelby stops by
with two blond honeys
the one driving reads my name tag
and says Case comeer
I run
no girl ever talks to me at Wood
except for Phyllis with the gold canines
on her way to work the NCO club
and the blond honey driving
asks me a motor vehicular question
I'm not prejudiced gainst cops
   I just loved her right away
but why would an MP
stop me going under the speed limit
I am about to reply with the sweetness and charm
before beauty when
on the incoming side of the gate
a beagle passing by attacks Wesley
I proceed to Wesley's assistance
but make a point not to swing my club
just to intimidate you know
and I hear one honey say to the other
look at that mean MP
tryin to beat on that dog
looks just like Buddy
and the blue gray Shelby leaves real fast

gin, Gregarian

all embarrassed he had to go to a maternity ward
to make a report of a beaten spouse
she just did not want to shut up says Gregarian
he never even knew what a period was
and the pregnant lady who'd miscarried
grossed him out
by the way his whore story from overseas
dealt with how well a girl could play cards
I explained it all to him and all kinds of things
became clear I think
he didn't say it out loud
but he was thinking it

churchkey

I hung out with Emanuel Klawir
and that's why Irish name aside
the Executive Sergeant Boddoms
had both of us on his list
he thought I was Jewish
we needed a bottle opener and Emanuel
goes into the liquor store off base
and asks for a synagogue key
guy right away gives him the opener
and I have a theory about this
there are so many Baptists in Missouri
when they go for beer
they too embarrassed to ask for a church key
they ask for a synagogue key instead
and the strict Baptists you know
they don't gamble either
you can bet on it

hook of Kerry

Kerry was a friend but also a thug
not the meanest kind but medium mean
the sergeants hated his guts and his friends
  and did you know there used to be seveneight
  neighborhoods in my town
   if you walked through em and you weren't Irish
   you'd get beat up and things are real bad now
   and there's only twothree neighborhoods like that
Emanuel and I get in between and stop
Kerry from beating the company clerk Lake
that particular friend of Executive Sergeant Boddoms
  I wanna hurt him Emanuel
  I really don't like him not at allll
  we'll fight   fair listen Lake show me ya moves
  no use stand against the wall t'hide I'll frame ya
  like a pitcher and hang you there
   you stupid fuck what moves do you have anyway?
Lake slimes out of it and then the three of us
Klawir Kerry and I get the call
to the First Sergeant for the accusation
of communicating a threat
and Kerry's there really in earshot of Top
going you should a let me punch him out Emanuel
I could have got him good
given him a hook around Casey's fat face

the guns of Bonnie or Clyde

Donohue our provost marshal's driver
gets to pay a courtesy visit
to the colonel in charge
of the Missouri State Highway Police
that colonel's driver is
not ugly like you Casey
but a peachy looking
young woman trooper
and Donohue brags
he got the tour
of the police museum
with Bonnie or Clyde weapons
and a free lunch
and did I know Bonnie and Clyde killed a couple of them
and for every willie AWOL deserter brought in
the Missouri Highway Police get a bounty
like a devil capturing souls I says
and John says of course
they have sneakers or boots mostly
not shoes

nuclear accident reaction force

there's the lad
sign right here on this line
verifies you received
twenty hours of hourly block training
in nuclear accident perimeter security

you wanted to see me First Sergeant

what is it you want signed?

gee I don't remember getting that training

where do I sign First Sergeant?

OK I guess we have to ask
Sergeant Boddoms here to give you
that training on your next forty-eight hours off duty
that's only nine days away
you can even prepare ahead of time
what's to know
tell the cars facing you
to go away
they can't enter the perimeter
and all the whilst your back side's
getting nucleated irradiated fried
you might even get a job
down the road as a nightlight
that might take twenty hours to learn
maybe more in your case

Mastrantonio and the rhinoceros beetle

Mastrantonio looks
and points at something on the ground
and yells
booo man hey wowww
look at that willya
that's a rhinoceros beetle
but I never seen one that big
I never seen one that ugly
it looks like Markham
when he wakes up in the morning
sheeit it looks like Markham
anytime a day
don't get too close
that can really hurt ya
gimme a pencil
gimme something it can latch onto
hey Markham gimme ya finger
and Markham gives Mastrantonio a finger

scairt

was I scared fuckin A
was he scared fuck no fuck no
what ever you say about him
short and round and very ugly
and extremely loud
y'sposed to be five ten
get into MP school no?
why'd I ever get stuck with him?
and those losers at Special Processing
were stealing stuff from the engineers
they was caught and then the fights
major lumps
and when we get there
bout twenty engineers
are walking with resolve
albeit slowly toward the scene
with bunk adapters entrenching tools
chains tire irons
my partner sees this
what does Einstein do
he brilliantly yells DROP IT
MILITARY POHLEECE
and everyone drops weapons
and books
yelling THE PEES THE PEES
so was he scared
while I am around
nobody says anything bad about him
but he's too fucking dumb to be scared
ignorant fuck the stupid fuck the dumb fuck

almost a star

one time Roes almost makes the stage
he is standing guard before the carnival platform
looking strak and every once in a while
catching a look of the stage behind him
the girl dancing away
looking fine and getting better and better
 and then it happens
she dancing all the time grabs his hat
and keeps it just out of reach
Henry is pretending to be a good sport
at least initially and jumps up and down
grasping for it from the orchestra pit
and that hat is always just out of reach
the audience laughs
and then she start rubbing the hat on her
all over her
and the audience roars
this is really enough for Henry
he tries to climb up on the stage
and she pushes him
he falls flat on his can
and the crowd is in a billion stitches
next day the manager of the carnival
asks the provost marshal specifically
for Roes to guard the stage once again
Henry Roes says to me
that breeder wants to make me
the object of larger ridicule
I says oh no
I don't think that at all

the bear

the carnival on base had its trained bear
motheaten and ancient
the thing kills its trainer
swipes the trainer good on the neck
and breaks something vital
though there was not much blood
no claws on the bear
no teeth for that matter
we again could not find the dog officer
and Lieutenant Davis bravely shot the bear
so the medics could go into the cage
get the trainer
next day someone steps
on a puppy at the carnival
the animal some poor kind of hound
a Lowell retriever
a prize at one of the games
and the poor thing was hurting
we again could not find the dog officer
Roes suggested we call for Lieutenant Davis
he the dog officer ipso facto aint he?

AGO

of course I remember you
the traffic accident
on the rainy night
those four willies did not have
a month's worth of service
total time in grade
I got a list of names
from the Provost Marshal's
to find someone anyone
who would have seen
that sergeant there that night
not drunk
and I saw your name on the list
not only did you not see him drunk
you did not see him period
you did not even see the car crash sight
you were twothree
hundred yards down the road
directing traffic
of course I remember you
I remember by the way
I got him off   the sergeant
effectively got him off
a fifty dollar fine and
four trainees dead in the rain

money truck

in the memory of some permanent party
there'd been a hold up of the PX money truck
with the receipts one evening
from the six PX's on Leonard Wood
and the then money truck driver
they found dead in a dumpster in Rolla
and some certain suspects at the time
were known to have businesses off base
hence an MP car
was assigned to follow the money truck
the MP escort was a Chevy Two cruiser
the oldest one at Wood
and the gears would stick
you actually had to open the hood
and move the gear with your fingers
there was no radio in the money truck
car four we called it
one time the escort car gets
stuck in first and car four drives off
while we are stopping to change gears
Wesley forgets car four doesn't have a radio
and he whispers over the radio
carfourholdup carfourholdup
and in like seconds
we are surrounded by everyone
the patrol supervisor and white hat patrols
the CI car the dog catcher
and even the Provost Marshal
jumping on Wesley's case
get it for improper word usage
thinks he's so smart
thinks he's
an English teacher something?

Chevy Two cruiser with double bubble

Wesley always impressed me
the razor fight scars on his face
he is permanent party for two months longer
than most of us new pees
once he parks the cruiser in the lot outside
the PMO at the top of the hill
and for a bit he and my friend Bill
take a break inside
they hate each other
and they are often
partners on patrol
with Wesley senior man
they go outside and no cruiser is in the lot
now the big field down hill
next door to the PMO
is all clear not a tree or boulder
or one discerning feature
but for at the bottom
in the center   a giant hole
and there's Wesley's cruiser
the back end sticking out of the hole
they ask Wesley what happened
and he says he doesn't know
so they ask Bill separately
and he says
I saw Lewis put on the emergency brake
which must have failed in some kind
of apparently mechanical misfunction
   Wesley Bill's new friend
tells me Bill thinks he so smart
because he is so smart
hang around
you might learn something
it's possible

razor cut

Wesley is talking to a Brother
and I walk toward them
Wesley say to him
homeboy Casey's from Baltimore
it's a joke
Wesley knows I'm from Boston
and the Brother leaves
  clearly something I said I says
  y'af to be so white says Wesley
  laugh Bro he says

the raid

the raid was a rumor for a while
and then the list was posted
people to report for duty
with clubs and forty-fives
and there's a conflict
I am on the list for KP
sixteen hours worth of pots and pans
when I am on the raid list too
Boddoms gets blamed for putting me on both lists
and the First Sergeant says I am a good lad
not wanting to miss out on the raid
what gung ho ass kicking pee burner
would want that eh? Boddoms?
and the DEA give us the pep talk
with blackboard diagrams maps and lists
so many people in each truck to each door
of the pot barracks
I am the first one out of my truck but I stumble a bit
just before I jump off
and so I do not so much jump as fall off
head first the crowd after me off the truck
steps and kicks and trips
over and on the unconscious me
the last guys off the truck
pick me up and throw me back on
I look like greater hell back at company
it's the only time Boddoms really smiles

patrol supervisor

in the company
the patrol supervisor sergeant
was one of the few married men
that did not stop him
from bushwhacking
he was the best at it
there with a flashlight
by the side of the parked car
eyes bulging with his lecture
  I am older and wiser than you
  and I will tell you
  here on a dirt road
  I would tell to you
  it is not a good idea
  for a female person
  to disrobe on an army base

ten ten the area

some women would get lonely
with husbands away
and call in frivolous made up complaints
Bill the radioman calls us
a prowler purportedly at the NCO housing area
and Roes driving the cruiser
was familiar with the caller
he really hauls to a house on Beauregard Street
streets there all named for rebels
we get to the housing area
and the patrol supervisor was there before us
he looks at us and he didn't seem
to want our help
he says I'll take care of this Roes
you and Klawir beat feet
ten ten the area

Davis and the lion

the brigade mascot breached
escaped from its half garage sized pen
I thought we'd never find it
though all cars were ordered to search
except the dog catcher
could never find him
oh we'll never find that catamount
I am thinking when I hear over the radio
close that blanking door
we do find it
hiding in a corner of the yard
at the base library
now Sergeant Tenewicz said his dogs would tree it
but there it is in the midst of two foot shrubs
so we try to herd it
into a portable cleaning cage
the lion looks at the cage
looks at Tenewicz' beagles
and jumps for Lieutenant Davis
Davis shoots it on the fly
with a forty-five no more and kilt it
even the dogs were impressed
they stopped barking
started whimpering
and then were quiet
and animals all over Missouri
were ascairt of Davis then on
lions and beagles and bears

OK this

OK this sergeant beats up his lady
we get the phone call to his house
on base housing
and bring him in
his company has to send
one very pissed off
officer to sign for him
and then the subject wifebeater
must stay at his company's orderly room
for twenty-four hours
before going back home

then we get frantic call from the company CQ
that one particular sergeant has broken
this twenty-four hour restriction
and run off
of course we suspect his worst
the desk sergeant phones the guy's house
the guy answers
and the desk sergeant asks
  is this sergeant wifebeater's house?
  is your wife home as we speak?
  sorry wrong number
and the MP cruiser arrives in time
the wife lets them in
and they find the sergeant
hiding in the bathroom
sort of around the toilet
from the cruiser leaving his yard
the sergeant gives his wife the finger
that really teaches her something

toothpick

in any vehicle
cab jeep three quarter ton
even in a cruiser
if you were at the window
and if Grant saw her
on the sidewalk
on your side
he'd nearly crawl over
two people to open the window
and yell TOOTHPICK
  gees I ask why you do that?
    it's fun
  do me a favor don't do that I says
    why shouldn't I
  because it hurts her feelings
    how do you know
    she never yells back

south gate

south gate was ten miles some
way from the main base
out of the boonies
I was never crazy over goin there
be honest with yis
sort of scary out there
all quiet no traffic hardly at all
phone rings and rings one night
while I am goin to the bathroom
and I finally answers it
    south gate PFC Urbi speakin

and the voice says
    Urbi this is Captain Brommelsick

      yessir Captain Brommelsick this is PFC Urbi

took you a long time to answer the phone dinit?

      yessir I was goin to the bathroom sir

you were sleepin weren you Urbi?

      nosir I weren sleepin sir

you lie'n to me Urbi

      nosir I wasn lie'n
      I would never lie to you sir
and then the voice starts laughin
and I know it all along

it weren Captain Brommelsick at all
it was Croft that no nuts Croft
I was so mad at him
he is really a mean person
wakin me up like that

south gate, Specialist Croft speaking

last night at south gate
the phone calls and in talking
to this irrevocably dumb someone
that moron someone hung up on me
admit it Urbi
it was you that called Urbi
who else'd call
when I'm at south gate
and try to pretend he's Captain Brommelsick
something to remember Urbi
when you are trying to pretend
you're Captain Brommelsick
on the phone
you say   this is Captain Brommelsick speaking
you don't say   this is Captain Urbi speaking

Croft uncentered

you don't expect anything
bother a loudmouth
and the news of his orders upset him
he had a two day pass shortly after
and I had a thought
he wouldn't be back
he was
I asked him
  your leave good?
he says oh God yeah
     I spent Saturday under a bridge
     with a twenty-two and one bullet
     worse thing? I had to borrow
     the twenty-two from Urbi
     you see any irony here?
     he believed me when
     I said I need target practice
     and the man gives me one bullet
     and a rifle without any bolt
     oh God it was great

the returnee

General Westmoreland said
there were too many pees in Nam
we'll make them grunts
and the fact that we were not trained
as infantry didn't matter
and so my battalion did tactical stuff
the garrison and patrolling
of a quiet district
but once in a while we'd find them
contact
I personally think
they were armed draft dodgers really
with third shelf weapons
no counts no contests
who the holy Jesus be scairt
of them dinks just running and hiding
when they weren't shooting you in the back

duty officer

after Diagati gets thrown out the window
he's crying at guardmount
because he doesn't want to be a stockade guard
I jump on his shit
tell him those boots better be shining better tomorrow
or hell is raised he never be white hat again
now it's engineers in the towers
so he can't go there
so I tell Tenewicz
have him guard the fire hydrant
in the workyard nights
five days of that he's AWOL
fuckin boredom worse'n fuckin fear
today's action army
even the military police desert

sally port

after the NCOIC
the duty officer talks
  nobody will get any article fifteens
  there will be no DR's
  no one will catch any shit whatever
  for beating on a prisoner
  is there anyone here
  too dumb to understand
  what that means?
and in all the guardmount
even the dimmest turnkey understood

stockade tower

the tower by the work yard
was manned daytimes only
nighttime the yard was closed off
Croft brought me over one dusk
I thought he was showing the view
and it was getting cool
but once up the tower
it's cold up here air-conditioned?
and Croft says
you know the guy killed the prisoner?
he jumped from here
not so high I says
his legs would brake the fall no?
no he goes the fall breaks his neck
there was a rope attached
let's scare Urbi up here I says
already did but he wasn't as scairt as you
said his auntie seen a ghost
sometimes it under her bed

Roes en passant

Roes says to a prisoner
just in passing
  you ever been to the loony bin
and the guy says
  many times
  understand never as a patient
he was only there at various institutes
visiting his nutso wife
and the last time
and the latest institute
he went with his girl friend
to see his old lady
and the institution wouldn't let them in
because get it
they was both barefoot
  c'mon y'know it is a loony bin
  understand people are mutes there
  and someone's in charge
  gonna worry about foot fungus?

patch of green

over the six foot patch of green
where prisoners generally don't go
they think it's a grave
in the middle of the stockade yard
we are talking the war up
Negroni and me
listening to Tenewicz saying
you have to have a war
you have such a big army
you need to do something with it
else it's a waste of money
and Negroni looks at him
says please go away
and then he Negroni leaves
the thing is that Negroni
is the one leaves goes back
into the barracks
where he's a prisoner
and Tenewicz and I are guards
this was maybe a month before Negroni's suicide
his wife left him
and the war had nothing to do with it
although maybe standing on
that green patch of grave
was not such a good move

my brother-in-law and me

my brother-in-law and me
we came back from work
with a case of beer
this was after working overtime
and we walk into the door
and I see my wife
sitting on the couch
with her bra and panties on
and this guy I never seen before
is standing in front of the TV
in his shorts
turning it on
I say to my brother-in-law
let's get out of here
and we walked out
we drunk the beer at his house

Manwarring's defenestration

the parolees just breached
some of them
but the maximum custody barracks
the box actually rioted
most of the guards there
made it to the turnkey
at the sally port gate but
Diagati and Manwarring
were guarding the upstairs
and did not wake up in time
from sleeping on empty bunks
so with the sound of breaking glass
and yelling and screaming
they the prisoners
threw Manwarring and Diagati
out the second floor windows
Diagati says
that he did not scream
like Manwarring
when they was throwed
out the window
but best be advised
you better believe
he yelled like hell

Jody

someone's being ironic
sometimes I don't get it
goes straight over my helmet liner
the girl I dated in college
two years beneath me
writes me says that since
I am not around
she's shacking up
with the boy
in the dorm
across the way
she writes this glibly
and is maybe using irony
thinking I'd like the sound
of something that sounds
so lousy to me?
but you know honestly
I don't like the fucking sound of that

when you says she's beneath you
she's beneath you in college?
does that mean she under you
I never been to college
I am not a specialist on this
but Sergeant Boddoms and I
not just pretend friends
to ya ugly face
want ya to know
we think ya college
is pretty fuckin nasty
oh I am hip
write sometimes
after ya knock yaself out
call me sometime
when ya wake up
good to know
she not gainsaying you ain it

military tattoo

left arm right arm
pairs of dice
drawn with no sense
of perspective whatever
boxcars various sevens
Grandma Moses drunk with ink
snake eyes elevens
all this illegal
your epidermis is
government property in the army
hand drawn tattoos in ballpoint
with safety pin artistry in the stockade
nobody would say or find out anything
if you can't see the art
or if such art does not fester
but lucky Ankybrant get his infected
who'd ever want a spider tattoo
on his face chasing
a fly tattoo under his hair
we all think the little shit
gets his bad luck on purpose

rumors ran along the valley

nine days on twelve hours a day two days off
and on my first day off
the company clerk run through the barracks
each pass cancelled everyone in fatigues
helmet liners and clubs in formation
in front of the orderly room
guess the box rioted in the stockade
elsewise we'd have weapons
but where's the breaking glass sound
now we had weapons raiding
the pot barracks no not enough people
get the cooks too
serious stick time the anticipation of
now Roes and Hoback
had already turned in their equipment
they show up on their own
not wanting to miss out on the fight
with baseball caps and bunk adapters
so what happened
it wasn't the prisoners rioting at all
it was the rumor
the St. Louis Committee
for Fair Play for Military Prisoners
was going to demonstrate at the main gate
we get to wait at the main gate
for eight hours
Roes and Hoback are excused
go back to their ready Vietnam training
Roes and Hoback laugh at us
it was a great joke

crash shatter

people off duty left early
so as not to be called for standby
call them standby evaders around here
but last night when these individuals came back
after movies or NCO clubs
that's when it started
the prisoners' breaking windows
everyone was called
they gave the cooks and clerks
MP helmets and clubs to bust heads
they had us rushing from barracks to barracks
with a firehose and so
a dozen twenty or so pees
no more maybe forty
and prisoners from other barracks
each yard ringed with its own wire
were cheering as prisoners from one barracks
were chased and clubbed
outside in their underwear
the fire hose was never turned on
once they yelled turn it on
and nothing happened
and another time they yell turn it on
and then a louder wait a minute
and maybe a quart of water drubbles out
and a prisoner walks by saying
everyone crazy here
someone have to mop that up

the hogtieing of Montgomery

Canney had a straw colored Villa mustache
reddish blond hair and beer gut
coaches told him lift weights and drink beer
concussed in a football game
he refused to play football again
and the college took away his scholarship
the draft happens and he has real nice words
to say about football coaches
with the loudest voice in the world
at the riot Canney yells
    they got you here Case?
    even white hats here?
    ain't this a hassle?
he points to a prisoner in front of the rioters
subject lighting matches one at a time
    see him that's Montgomery
    one strong little dude
    we brought him back from the hospital
    little dude got his arms free and biff
    right between my eyes ouuhh
    I saw little stars like in cartoons
    only more plentiful you know
    watch now we gonna put him
    in a non transient condition

SNAKEGGS

this is it Kerry the boxer
knows how to arrange
a couple of twisted paperclips
and a big really big elastic in a envelope
a business size envelope on which are big letters
RATTLE SNAKEGGS
the result is a really bulky looking envelope
that he places on
the clerk's desk in the orderly room
right where everyone walks by
including that major prick Boddoms
so this is it
Boddoms walks by
sees the envelope and the nosy little shit
discretely picks it up
and the elastic snaps like a gunshot against the paper
and scares the corn
out of the shit
out of Boddoms who jumps back
and he is royally pissed
but it is beauteeful
he can't act pissed
because the first sergeant was in on it
and Top is laughing like anything
and Boddoms is really ripping mad inside
but trying like to act the good sport
wondering how to get even with Kerry
and then my good friend Kerry
puts in a good word
he says I got the envelope from Casey

hammer and snath

Sergeant Tenewicz says
to get some tools from the work yard
so I go there
and when I get back to one fifty-five
medium custody stockade barracks
I have five grass sickles
not scythes snaths or grass whips
but the small hand tools
like half the logo on the Soviet flag
and Tenewicz looks at them says
whadya nuts? get them the fuck out a here
y'want those gooks t'get rice knives?
it's the first time hear prisoners called gooks
and sickles called rice knives

Tenewicz at courts martial

the witness Tenewicz is messed
got a nervous facial twitch
a bad stutter
keeps trying to light a cigarette
and apologizing for forgetting
that he can't light up
has a total unrecall of events
and a voice too loud in a small room
   the defendant had worked in the stockade
   two weeks before deserting
   and how long had the sergeant worked at the stockade?
      five years there I worked
      at the correctional facility there sir
   and how many times had the sergeant gone AWOL
the civilian defense lawyer is going nuts
but Tenewicz goes honest
      sir long ago should have gone long ago
      but since I beat up on prisoners now
      it don't bother me much as before sir

transfer request

I thought I'd talk to just
the first sergeant about it
   you sure you want to do this
   of course it might be over
   before you get there
but of course Boddoms was near by
      of course it'll still be going on
      so you want to die
      so you want to go bangbang
      maybe it's boomboom you want
I shook hands with both of them
thanked Top for getting
my handcuffs back
from the CI guy that stole them
and I told Boddoms
I want to be like him
when I grow up

beaujolais

Devine the chemist hears about my orders
my ready Vietnam training
and he calls me over to drink wine
coke cans for glasses
the tops cut off
and the sharp edges pounded smooth
he's nuts about this wine
    I didn't expect to find beaujolais in Waynesville
this is a superb wine
    it certainly is   I am surprised too
    it is like finding frascati here you know
    almost as rare in Missouri   I says
but see he invited Karl Beeson the physicist
and Kerry the boxer
and the thing was
it was only a half bottle to begin with
really I felt like getting drunk
which was difficult to do
on one quarter of a half bottle of beaujolais

Sp/4 West

all the others from my MP school class
levied out and replaced by new people
from Fort Gordon
I was older than most
and thought wiser
the new people would ask me for advice
common sense stuff mostly
even for the lonely sick of heart
after Urbi's fight with a girlfriend
I said write to her
say you miss her letters and you hope
her broken writing hand has healed
and would like to see her again
it worked but then
some situations were more involved
Urbi refers Johnstone to me
a girl sent Johnstone a mystery letter
and he thought it meant
she was pregnant
and Johnstone was pissed
I explain it carefully
he'd misread the correspondence
that in fact the something
she thought he might have given her
was not a baby
but a venereal disease
should have seen Johnstone's happy face
that his girl had his VD
instead of his baby
what a lucky girl

Wilkison Sword

so what kind of fool would desert the army
in Germany go to Sweden
where there are so many blond girls
that brunettes have more fun
and come back to Ft. Wood Missouri
Fort Lost-in-Woods Misery
a guy who worked for Gene McCarthy
on the Chicago convention floor
I heard about him when I was white hat
and then as a stockade guard
I am having words with one prisoner
he asks me where I'm from
and I tell him and he says he'll be at my house
when the army is over and get even with me
and it's the same fool
half my size threatening me
and it's his mother who leads
the St. Louis Committee for Fair Play
for Military Prisoners
only when I am on ready Vietnam training
at the automatic fire range
guess who is my scorer   the fool
he forgot his part of the threat then
and I forgot the other half
so two fools who worked for Eugene McCarthy
were on the rifle range
we wondered how we could lose
we were so sincere

letter from Fagan

I'd wrote him about my levy order and
while his first letters had a return address
Co B 2/327 1st Bde
101 Airborne
APO SF 96383
the word free on the upper right corner
no stamp
the last letter did have a stamp
American
the return address
Ward 4
7th Field Hospital
APO SF 96344

he'd dug a hole to hide in
but didn't want to sleep in it
and then the perimeter was mortared
as he was hauling ass for his pit
the better to fight in   crossed out
to wallow in fear in which   inserted
when he was scratched on the side
and the next thing
a wake up not in a pit
but on a hospital bed in Japan
the fifty-first state the free world
three hundred sixty yen to the dollar
must have been quite a scratch
he wrote   fuck the high ground
keep your ass down
they tell you
do something stupid
don't

AG Levy

two troops from the AG Levy section
got into an accident
a fender bending
each guy looked and didn't see the other guy
the left front corner of one car
hit the right front corner of the other
what to do
Diagati and I
gave them each a ticket
one for careless and reckless driving
contributing to a traffic accident and
one for careless and reckless driving
causing a traffic accident
later ten of us from the 208th
Military Police Company get notices
from the Adjutant General Levy Section
a levy calls us for overseas duty
eight of us to go to Korea
Diagati and I begin ready Vietnam training
at the automatic fire range we discuss it
Diagati says he has nothing to worry about
his name mean God guards
he asks me what my name means

bus stop

I am waiting at the bus stop on base
and who should arrive by
but Specialist Manwarring
I remember Manwarring in a bad way
stammering and his face all scarred
for being throwed out
the second floor window
of a stockade barracks
now though in the patrol car
as senior man white hat
he was big time
a recent MP School grad as a lackey
he says   old times sake   Case
we give y'a ride
the guided tour of Fort Leonard Wood
I says I don't know Man
I mean I'm waiting for a bus out a here
and he goes
c'mon nothing ever happens
so I go for ride and get stuck in an emergency call
to OPC General Leonard Wood Army Hospital
for a reported dog bite
I miss my scheduled bus
of course I get the next bus three hours later
but it was that much later
and only one seat was left
next to an Englishman on tour it were
he tried to relate to me
with coarse language and all
you have a fookin woonderful country

Jody the Brit

Englishman next to me on the bus
sees my white hat in a baggy
and asks
  an officer?
I says
  no enlisted
and he goes
  ah one of the lower orders
he notices that I am upset and explains
that the expression is theological
referring to the clergy in his country
the lesser rank and the expression
is not rhizopodic or protozoal at all
his girlfriend next to him on the other side
is an American with an Irish name
she giggles a lot I cannot but think
should he not move out
go back where he comes
and take her with him
I would have